Drama-Free Zone

How to Deal With Conflict at Work

(Coaching For Success Series, Book 2)

by Mark A. Baggesen

Title: Drama-Free Zone

Subtitle: How to Deal With Conflict at Work

Disclaimer and FTC Notice

Cover designed by Romana Bovan. Contact/Portfolio: 99designs.com/profiles/246674

Find Mark A. Baggesen at: https://coachyourselfbooks.com

ISBN13: 9781698311814

Dedication

May your life be happy and your work drama-free.

Table of Contents

Preface

"Drama starts where logic ends."

~ Ram Charan, Actor

Drama

Definition of drama. 1a literature: a composition in verse or prose intended to portray life or character or to tell a story usually involving conflicts and emotions through action and dialog and typically designed for theatrical performance: play - compare closet drama.

~ Merriam-Webster Dictionary

Question: Is that what you want in your workplace?

No?

I didn't think so.

Drama is fine for movies, plays, television shows and in your personal life (as much of it as you can stand). However, drama has no place in the professional work environment. People who create, enable and build drama in the workplace are drama queens, manipulators, unhappy people, and those unable to control their emotions or they have other agendas than getting work done. Some people revel in creating upheaval and discord; they revel in being the center of attention. But drama in the workplace is annoying, upsetting, distracting and unproductive. It is an unnecessary problem. And yet, it's still a factor today.

Unless you are part of a stage or film performance, there should be no drama in your workplace.

Over the last 25 years I have looked for the peace available in a place I call the "drama-free zone." I have created that zone for myself, peers, managers and employees. Never in that time, has anyone complained to me about the negative effects of the "drama-free zone."

This book will teach you how to create your own drama-free zones.

If you're looking for a book about how to create more drama, this book is not for you.

Note: there is no definition in any dictionary I can find for "drama-free." Interesting, isn't it?

About Me and this Book

I have been in middle and senior management for the last 25 years for Fortune 500 companies. I am an expert at turning chaos into order and success, recovering failed technology projects and complex problem solving. My work is my play and I enjoy it immensely.

Wouldn't it be nice if everyone's work was their play? That's what you get when you work in a drama-free zone. A drama-free zone does not mean an area with no emotion. It is a space with no negative emotions or unnecessary distractions that cause conflict.

If this book is helpful to you, maybe you will share it with others or show them how to create their own drama-free zones.

In a world that has so much daily vitriol, divisiveness, partisanship and rancor, wouldn't it be nice to experience a little peace of mind? Wouldn't it be nice to work in a drama-free zone?

Preparation

Consider using a notebook to write your answers to all the questions in this book. It could be a composition book or a loose-leaf notebook. It doesn't matter. What matters is that you answer all questions honestly and fully. This is the best way that this book can be helpful for you.

I have a gift for you: A hyperlinked list of additional resources you can read on each subject discussed in this book. You can download this file for free on my website (https://coachyourselfbooks.com/worksheets/)

I recommend that you read this whole book through first (in a few days' time). Afterwards you can go back and work through each chapter (in a few weeks). Allow yourself time and space to think about what you have read, then answer the questions meaningfully. This book is for you. You are worth the time!

Chapter 1:
Create a Drama-Free Zone for Yourself

It is better to conquer yourself than to win a thousand battles.
Then the victory is yours. It cannot be taken from you...

~ Buddha

Mark A. Baggesen

Start with Peace

"Peace is the beauty of life. It is sunshine. It is the smile of a child."

~ Menachem Begin, Israeli Politician

Peace

Each day is an opportunity to start anew. Or as the saying goes: "every day above the grass is a good one." Having peace in your life is essential to realizing a drama-free zone at work and in your life.

For some people, finding peace is not a problem: they're happily living their lives and content with their lot. For others, finding peace is difficult. Every day is a challenge. There are problems at home, the traffic that day was horrible, they drank too much caffeine, their glass is half empty or maybe they are just an unhappy person.

Whatever the cause, if you are one of these people or just having a bad morning, starting each day with a peaceful, positive state of mind will be revolutionary. Each person responds to stimuli differently. Each person may get into a peaceful state of mind by different means. The important thing is to get into that state of mind before you start your workday.

You know yourself. You know what makes you angry, stressed, happy or relaxed. Only you can decide what it will take to get into the right state of mind each morning before work. If you can't think of why you are not in this state, you will need to search for what will help you find that calm, that peace.

First Thing in the Morning

Mornings are something you like or something you dislike. Either way, it's important that you start your day well. If you begin your day as a grump, you may be that way until lunch or later. Here are some actions you can take, if you're a person who hates mornings.

Order and Routine - Having the same routine to what you do every day when you wake up and get ready for the day will make the morning easier. You will already know before you wake what you will do and when. All you have to do is get started.

For some people, exercise is good in the morning - If you haven't tried that, you might do some simple exercises or a short walk along with deep breathing exercises and see how you feel, especially if you're not in a positive mood. It doesn't take miles of walking to change a person's frame of mind, it just takes 10 to 15 minutes of movement.

For some people, meditation - If you wake up to lots of noise or thoughts of things to do, meditation may be helpful. There are free tools like the Headspace mobile app and others that can lead you to a calm and quiet state of mindfulness. Alternatively, you can spend 10 to 15 minutes sitting quietly while focusing only on your breathing and listening to the surrounding quiet. If that doesn't work, you might try headphones and loud rock and rock. For some people, loud music blasts away all the noise or thoughts and leaves them feeling relaxed and back in the zone.

Eat Something - if you're "running on empty" from the night before, chances are that your body needs energy. Eating something will help feed the body, stabilize the blood sugar and get you going. Eating something doesn't mean just coffee. Eating something means food: protein, carbs, dairy, whatever works for you.

For most people, drink water - Never underestimate the value of drinking a glass of water the first thing in the morning. No one drinks water while sleeping, yet every physical action burns off water from the body, even sleeping. An 8 ounce glass of water in the morning will help you, it definitely will not harm you.

The Drive to Work

There are few things as stressful as driving in rush hour

traffic. Some people pretend they are race car drivers, some are oblivious to anything going on around them, others wander between lanes while looking at their text messages and some drive close enough to your back bumper they could adjust the headrest for you.

If you've started your day well, driving to work does not have to ruin it. It's a matter of perspective. The perspective is: I want to get from Point A to Point B safely, with no drama, in a reasonable amount of time.

How do you achieve Point A to B without drama? Here are some thoughts:

Don't drive in the left lane, except for passing - Stay in the right or middle lane and just allow the traffic that's faster than you to go around on either side of your vehicle. It's not a race, don't buy into the idea that it is a competition. Note: If you hug the left lane and drive the speed limit, you'll only annoy people and may cause some accidents.

Don't cut others off - If you avoid the game of "I will move up in my lane, so you can't get in front of me," you'll be much happier and less stressed and so will other people. When drivers want to get into your lane, regardless of whether they use a turn signal, just let them in front of you and adjust your distance back a car length or two.

Learn to merge - when two lanes turn into one, that's called a "merge." Wait your turn and move along. Traffic will move faster than you can imagine, if you do this.

Be courteous - This shouldn't need an explanation, but: drive like there are other people on the road that have as much right to be there as you do. You don't own the road. No one does.

Listen to music you like - Listening to music is a great way to stay in the zone. Whatever style and volume of music you like is what will work for you.

Put the phone down or away - Don't be one of those people that looks at their phone while driving. It's annoying, dangerous and you're just asking for trouble. People who look at phones and drive appear to be driving drunk. This activity is so bad and widespread that states are passing new laws to criminalize using digital devices while driving. The National Safety Council estimates that 3,000 to 6,000 deaths a year in the United States are because of phone use while driving.

The world will not stop if you don't look at your phone. And no, the president is not calling you. And even if he is, he can leave a message like everyone else.

If you have done it right (the drive), when you arrive at work, you should be ready for the day's work. If you've driven well, you won't need time to recover from rush hour. If you have to recover from the drive to work, that's probably a sign you're doing it wrong and creating unnecessary drama on the road or that someone created it for you.

Summary

- Creating a drama-free work zone, starts when you wake up.
- If you are not a morning person, there are things you can do to make it better.
- The drive to work should not be a race.
- You should arrive at work ready to begin the day.

Questions to Ask Yourself

- Am I a "morning person?" If not, what can I do to improve my morning experience?
- What is my stress level in the morning? If it's moderate

or high what can I do to change that?

- Does driving in rush hour traffic stress me out? If yes, how can I make the drive better and less stressful?

- Am I a reckless driver that does careless things on the road? If yes, why?

- What else can I do, before the workday starts, to get in the right frame of mind?

Eliminate Distractions

"Almost all accidents take place because of human distraction."

~ *Sebastian Thrun, German Entrepreneur*

Concentration & Distractions

One thing that can totally mess up a drama-free zone is the lack of concentration. Often this happens because of distractions in the environment that keep you from being able to focus on work. Sometimes you create distractions, sometimes others create those. According to experts, it takes about 23 minutes for people to re-focus after being distracted. If you're distracted 4 or 5 times a day, that can blow up your whole day!

Here are some distractions you can control:

Checking Email - If you are checking your email every 5 or 10 minutes, you are distracting yourself and honestly wasting a lot of time and brainpower. Close your email. Check it twice in the morning and twice in the afternoon. If someone needs to get a hold of you, there is the telephone or they can stop by your office.

Cell Phone - It's easy to pick up the cell phone, to scan through personal email and the news, but this likewise is a huge waste of time. You should limit yourself to looking at your phone at lunch and after work.

Social Media - Being social used to mean speaking with someone face to face. Now it's totally out of control and can be a day long distraction. Take back the control: shut off notifications on your cell phone and check social media at lunch and after work. That way you can speak to people on your terms, in your timeframe and you will not be a slave to social media.

Browsing the Internet - Yes, you have a computer and yes the Internet is available to you via an Internet browser. That doesn't mean you should look at non-work related things on the Internet (all companies track Internet activity through their proxy servers and networks anyway). Not only is this a waste of time, but if your boss sees you surfing the Internet, what do you think she will think about that? It's estimated that the average employee spends up to 12 hours a week on non-work related Internet browsing, emails, social media and messaging (That's 25% of the work week) - imagine not only the loss of productivity for the employer, but the difficulty of the employee to concentrate on work. If you owned the company, would you want to be paying for that?

Your Desk - Is your desk a mess? Yes? Then it is a distraction. You may find everything, but that doesn't mean it's not a distraction. Clean up your desk and make it orderly. That will be one less distraction. You should be able to find whatever you need without digging through piles of paper. Who knows what you'll find when you clean.

Multi-tasking - There is a widely spread fallacy in our society that people can "multi-task" or do more than one thing at a time. That is false. Only computers can do more than one thing at a time. People move from one task to the other and back again - that's not multi-tasking. Constantly switching between different tasks will make you less efficient while taking more time. It is better to block time to do one task. When you complete that task, proceed on to the next one.

Unproductive Meetings - Nothing says "distraction" like wasting an hour or two in a poorly run meeting that results in no action items or agreements. Does anyone like these meetings? If you need to get your work done but meetings eat up a lot of your day, start blocking time on your calendar for work, as if those were meetings. It doesn't always work, but often if people see that your calendar is full, they won't schedule unnecessary meetings and will find another way to communicate with you.

Loud people near you - Depending on your workplace, you may have a cubicle with a high or low wall or an office with a door. If you have a door, and someone is too loud, just close the door. If you are outside of a conference room and people are in there talking loudly with the door open, likewise, quietly close that door. If you're in an open office environment, people should know when they are being too loud. If they don't, the next action is your choice. You can do nothing or you can either ask them nicely to talk quieter or go to a conference area. Also, you can put on your headphones and listen to music that only works if music helps you concentrate. Otherwise, you are trading one distraction for another.

Dozens - There might be dozens of other distractions in the workplace, but it's you that must take control, when possible, to remove those distractions so you can get your work done. What's the alternative, taking work home to do later? That's not a good solution.

Summary

- You should eliminate distractions to better focus on your day and work.

Questions to Ask Yourself

- Am I often distracted at work? If yes, are these distractions things that I can control?

- Are other people distracted at work or only me? If others are not, what are their secrets for staying focused? Why am I the only one distracted?

- Where are there more distractions: at home or at work? What mechanisms work for you to reduce these?

Emotion

"When dealing with people, remember you are not dealing with creatures of logic, but creatures of emotion."

~ *Dale Carnegie, Writer and Lecturer*

Negative Emotions

Negative emotion is the cause for much of the workplace drama. Emotions like worry, anxiety and anger can destroy you and those around you. Once these emotions are in the workplace, it's difficult to remove their effect on others.

When you think of a drama-free zone, think of a smooth, straight road in the California desert on a calm sunny afternoon. You can see as far as the next mountain range that is 20 to 50 miles away. Driving is effortless, stress free and predictable. Unless something like an earthquake happens, your trip along this road will be uneventful. It doesn't seem to matter if you drive at 40 miles per hour or 80-the experience will be the same.

Unfortunately, life and work is not a smooth road in the desert. It's more like a road with curves, potholes and hazards man-made (like trash) or natural (like a deer darting across the path). One thing is certain: life and work are not predictable or stress free.

No one can control the emotion of others - this you must accept. However, you can control your emotion and reaction to other's actions, events and unpredictable situations. This ability is a matter of training. In the Army, they call this technique adapt and react: something in a scenario happens (someone shoots at you); you adapt (by seeking cover behind a rock) and react (fire back at them). The point is, we can't act the same way all the time, but our response should be appropriate to the situation. If you learn to adapt and react, this skill will serve you well in both work and life.

People who know and use an "appropriate response" will be in control of a situation. People that cannot navigate that way will be at a disadvantage. For example, why would you use a hammer to put a thumbtack into a wall?

Again, positive emotions are good, but any other emotion in the workplace only creates drama.

Happiness

When at work are you happy or unhappy? Your state of mind really matters. It's very difficult to concentrate, do one's work and be highly productive, when unhappy.

If you are unhappy, where do you look for happiness? Do you look to others and outside things to make yourself content? Hopefully, your answer is no, you know why you're happy or unhappy.

If however, you're unhappy and look to other people or things for happiness or contentment, you will be disappointed and unhappy. Happiness comes from within, not from outside of you. Happiness in the workplace is a choice you make each day. If you think anything else, it will not help you.

Sources of happiness come from internal personal motivators such as satisfaction, amusement, challenge and success. If you are not happy at work, you need to figure out why.

In your personal life are you happy? The same principle applies: it's all about how you see the world and your place in it. You can choose to be happy.

Again, looking to others and outside things for happiness will not create happiness. It is the fulfillment of the fallacy "the grass is always greener on the other side." For example, you're unhappy at your job, so you get another one. After a short time, you find you are no happier at the new job. The situation is no better, it's just different. Since you didn't find the reason for your unhappiness at the first job, you are again unhappy at the second one.

If you're not happy, how can you change that? Here are a few ideas:

Choose happiness at work - There's a line in a Lyle Lovett song that says "I love everybody, especially me." Be happy with yourself. A little PMA (positive mental attitude) goes a long way. Think about positive things. Focus on the things about your job you like and enjoy. Avoid negative people and the gossip that is always churning somewhere in the office.

Do what you love every day - Make a point of doing something you love every day. It could be a task at work, it could be a lot of different things. Think about whatever gives you a feeling of satisfaction or fulfillment. That's a good place to start. Even if you don't like your job, you can find something that will give you joy.

Control your professional development - Do something one hour a day to improve your personal or professional skill set. Learning new things can be very gratifying and life affirming. Life does not stand still. You and your career should not stand still either.

Remove your own roadblocks - Are there things or situations that impede you from accomplishing your work? You can go to your manager and ask for help, or you can first try to solve those issues yourself. The enjoyment you can get from finding solutions to problems can be very satisfying.

Be grateful - Being grateful for your health, your job, your family and your life is very important. Verbally expressing gratefulness to yourself daily, can be a motivator and reinforcement of how lucky you are. The old cliché is true: we don't appreciate what we have until it's gone.

Stop thinking about what you don't have - You are not your possessions, your job, nor the vacation you can't afford today. You are much more than that. What you don't have, is what you don't have - stop thinking about it. Comparing yourself to others is stupid, self-defeating and a negative self-fulfilling prophecy. You can always turn a negative into a positive by setting goals for the things you want in life and working towards those goals. That way, those positive goals become something to look forward to.

Pay attention to what is going on - Not everyone knows what is happening around them at work. This is both unfortunate and short-sighted. Some say ignorance is bliss. Ignorance is not bliss, it's just ignorance. If you don't really know what is going on, pay attention so you always understand the environment. That will give you a sense of comfort and an advantage.

Ask for Feedback - Asking for feedback from your "customers" and your boss is an opportunity to see your strengths and positive abilities through their eyes and to learn what you need to work on next. Put on your adult pants, thicken your skin and ask for feedback from others. Don't be afraid to ask: What did you think about my contribution to the last project I worked on? How would you rate the quality of my work? What do you think I could improve on? Being acknowledged for good work is always a morale booster. Knowing what others think is paramount to your long-term growth and success.

Only commit to tasks you can complete - Too many people don't know how to negotiate their responsibilities with management. They keep taking on more work - more than they can ever complete. Don't do that. Only make commitments you can keep. That way, each achievement is a positive accomplishment for you and it will meet or exceed your manager's expectation. Your manager will also respect you for knowing your capabilities and limitations.

Avoid negativity - Some people are just not happy about anything. You need to know when and how to avoid those people and any situation that is not helpful to your psyche. Otherwise, you may get sucked into the same black hole. If you avoid those people and negative situations, it will really help. If you get sucked into the black hole of a negative mindset, it could ruin your whole day, week, life or career.

Build relationships with colleagues - Being pleasant, happy and sharing that with others in the workplace can be a great way to develop professional relationships at work. Get to know the people you work with. Colleagues will also think well of you because you're always so positive. A social network at work can provide support, resources, empathy and joy when you need it. The added benefit is that you will better understand the social workplace dynamics, and which people to avoid.

Your choice - As stated at the beginning of this section, you know what makes you happy and unhappy so do something about it. The alternative is not productive for you or for those around you.

Despite what some cynics say "happiness is not overrated." Happiness is under-utilized.

Summary

- Happiness comes from within. If you are looking for it anywhere else, you are looking in the wrong place.

Questions to Ask Yourself

- Am I happy at work? If not, why not? What can I do to feel better?

- Am I happy in my personal life? If not, why not? What can I do different to feel better?

- Do I do something I love every day? If not, why not?

- What things do I love to do? Make a list.

- Do I work on my professional development for one hour each day?

- Am I grateful for what I have? If not, why not?

- Do I often think about what I don't have or what I have? Why?

- Do roadblocks or obstacles stop my work? If so, when is the last time I tried to solve that problem myself?

- Do I have a genuine understanding of what is going on around me in the workplace, within my organization and company? If not, why not?

- When is the last time I asked for sincere feedback from my boss or clients/customers/peers?

- Do I over-commit to tasks from my boss and then end up not getting everything accomplished or driving myself to burnout? If so, how well is that working for me? What would work better?

- Do I often find myself stuck talking to people about negative things? If so, is that really helping me?

- Have I cultivated good relationships with my work colleagues? If no, why not? If yes, how has that helped me to be happier and to work better?

- What else could make me happier today? Why am I not doing it yet?

Worry and Stress

Worry and stress can all work together in a vicious cycle difficult to stop. These can create significant drama in both the workplace and in one's personal life. The following section looks at these and what you can do.

Worry is a destructive emotion. It is so strong that it can literally make people sick. Chronic worry is not good for anyone. Consider this: most things people worry about NEVER happen!

Think of this simple view of worry: worry is a zero or a one. If it's a zero and you can't do anything about it, why worry? If it's a one, and you can do something about it, what are you waiting for? Do something about it. If that works for you great! For some people, this is just too simple a solution to a problem that causes them lifelong, considerable agony.

Chronic worrying can affect people in many ways: loss of appetite, a change in relationships, sleep difficulty and erratic job performance. Physically, worry can cause illnesses that range from headaches to heart attacks in extreme cases.

Here are some things you can do to attack worry:

Understand what is causing worry, then try to do something about it. There's a lot of misinformation out there about worry. For example, you may think: "If I worry that something bad will happen, nothing bad will happen." That's not true, but the more times you tell yourself that thought (and nothing bad happens), the more you will believe it.

Embrace uncertainty - Life is uncertain, regardless of your age, your income, your location or your ethnicity. Try to accept and embrace that fact. If you do, you will find that it may not bother you as much. As one person said "just roll with it." Life can be chaos, but when it is, learn to live with it (by knowing it will not always be that way). Whatever your worries, know that most of these will never happen.

Live in the present - People who worry, do so because they are thinking of something that could happen in the future. People do not worry about what's happening now. So, if you live in the present (also called mindfulness), you can enjoy the here and now. Something may or may not happen. Either way, it is not happening now.

Face your fears - Nothing says "you've got game" like facing what you are afraid of. Most fears are irrational: the dark, heights, money, health, car accidents, train accidents, plane accidents - oh my! You can either live with these fears for your entire life, or you can face them. Which would you prefer? If you face your fears, they will disappear like dust in the wind. You might not believe it now, but fear really is all you have to be afraid of.

Exercise daily – It is scientifically proven that moderate daily exercise releases chemicals in the body that help people reduce their worry and stress and anxiety issues (Oddly enough, so does hot, super spicy food). If you exercise daily, then you know how that makes you feel. Regular aerobic and strengthening exercises can provide measurable relief. The key here is "doctor approved" and moderation. Start with an easy exercise session and increase it over time to a moderate level that's safe, but that challenges your body. You will become stronger, healthier and worry less.

Talk to your doctor – Your doctor can give you a physical exam to make sure this worry is not caused by a physical condition. She can also prescribe other treatments or medicines.

If you typically worry in silence, this could be an opportunity to talk with someone you trust. The action of talking with someone may help reduce worry.

Limit Your Caffeine and Stimulants – Coffee, tea, sodas and other foods have caffeine or stimulants in them. There are many kinds of stimulants. These include coffee, nicotine, over-the-counter decongestants and many others. If you use too many of these, it can negatively affect your body and heighten the feeling of worry. If you are a worrier, limit your caffeine/stimulants and observe if you feel better. Many people have issues with stimulants, but since coffee, other foods and over-the-counter medicines are part of modern culture, people ignore these as contributing factors in mental health. You may find that you feel better and can focus acutely without stimulants.

Stress

Stress is the physical and mental reaction created by your brain and body when things happen in life. Some stress is good and can help you focus and perform well during the day. Too much stress can cause your body to go into "fight or flight" mode. This is an ancient, innate response that helps humans solve real physical threats (like being chased by a saber-toothed tiger in prehistory). If "fight or flight" mode happens at the wrong time or often without cause, that's when you should look for solutions.

The human brain is hard-wired to react to stimuli. For example, if someone points a gun at you, your brain will react by releasing hormones into your body to increase your heart rate and blood pressure, so you can react quickly to the threat. That's a normal physical response. What is not normal is when there is no threat and your brain fires up the "fight or flight" mode and it does not go away by itself.

The emotional symptoms of excessive stress include

irritability, depression, anxiety, low sex drive, memory and concentration problems, mood swings and compulsive or unpredictable behaviors.

According to an Ipsos poll of December 2018, 64% of Americans are stressed at work. Half of those people say it is negatively affecting their life. That's one-third of the workforce! Are you one of them?

Stress Management

Stress management is how people treat stress in their life. Sometimes doctors prescribe medication, if the emotion becomes more than stress management can treat.

The good news is that almost everyone benefits from stress management. Relaxation techniques such as meditation, walking, jogging or sports can help to slow breathing and focus attention. These techniques can break the stress cycle by creating the adult equivalent of a mental "timeout."

Summary

- Worry is a terrible emotion, but it can be treated. The sooner you deal with the worry, the sooner you will find relief.

- Stress is a normal part of life. If stress is causing you problems, there are things you can do to improve how you feel.

Questions to Ask Yourself

- Do I worry about things that may happen in the future? If so, how well is that working for me?

- Does worry keep me from being able to make decisions (i.e., analysis paralysis)?

- Do I know someone that worries? If so, what has worry

done for them?

- Do I know anyone that used to worry? If so, how did they solve this problem?

- Do I experience anxiety that does not go away after a situation? If so, what have I done so far to treat it?

- Do I experience normal or excessive stress daily? If yes, have I spoken to someone that I trust about it?

Mark A. Baggesen

People

"Catch on fire and people will come for miles to see you burn."

~ John Wesley, Clergyman, 1703 - 1791

It's All About the People

There is an excellent book by Ronna Lichtenberg titled "Work Would Be Great If It Weren't For The People." This title says it all for many workplaces and many social situations. People make the workplace difficult. The work itself is usually not what makes the workplace problematic. People cause the drama, only people can remove it.

If you work for a manager that creates drama, that's unfortunate. If you are a manager that creates drama, know this: People don't quit companies, they quit managers (people).

You must understand one thing: if you work in a company, you don't choose who you work with, who you work for and rarely who works for you. If you accept a job with an organization, that's usually the last time you'll make a personal decision about the people. Therefore, during the interview process it is very important to ask the right questions, to speak with a wide variety of people in the group and to research on Internet sites like Indeed.com, Linkedin.com and Glassdoor.com to understand the people, the environment, the culture and its challenges.

For example, if you have an interview and find that people have stayed with this manager for 10 years, that speaks volumes for the manager. If you find that all the employees are only 1 to 2 years (or less) into the job, you need to ask why. Is this a new department? Or is this only a new team headed by the same manager? What happened to the last team he managed?

People will always be a factor in your workplace.

Acquaintances Are Not Friends

People at work are not friends. People at work are acquaintances. You definitely don't know them, what they really think, what they do in their off hours and what they want in life. Acquaintances are not friends, they are people you barely know.

Here's a definition from Merriam Webster for your edification:

Acquaintance: *A person one knows slightly, but who is not a close friend. As in "a wide circle of friends and acquaintances" or*

"Mr. Barnet was no more than a business acquaintance."

~ www.lexico.com

With people you do not know, you can only share so much of yourself. You must be on guard of what you say, do and how you act in their presence. Again, they are not your friends. If you remember this, it will serve you well. The easiest way to practice this is to consider everyone you work with your customer or client. How would they like to be treated? What would they like and not like to know or hear from you?

Here's an analogy about acquaintances: every interaction of yours with people, your mother is watching you. If you do something your mother does not approve of, what usually happens? Right, she corrects you or slaps your hand. In reality, however, your mother is not in the workplace. The repercussions of what you say, do or how you act come from other people. Unlike your mother, their reactions may be unpredictable and more severe.

What You Control

People will do what they have always done. Some are good, some are bad. Either way, you can change no one. You can only control what you can control: your behavior and your reaction to people. To illustrate my point here is what Albert Einstein said about married couples: "Man marries woman hoping she will not change. Woman marries man hoping he will change. Invariably, both are disappointed."

If your workplace is bad, what should you do? For many people, especially Millennials, the answer is "find another workplace." Millennials don't put up with difficult company cultures. They float between jobs like butterflies, when unhappy.

For the rest of us, the answer is more complex. There appear to be 3 choices:

- Work within the company to make things better

- Accept the situation and make the best of it

- Leave

Many people go for option two and make the best of a difficult situation. They bide their time, bite their lip and wait for a chance to move. Depending on how toxic the workplace is, that might be a reasonable solution. If the workplace is only unpleasant, know that there are worse ones out there. Staying at that job is not necessarily the wrong answer.

However, if the workplace is toxic, meaning lots of drama, micromanaging clueless management, long hours and poor attitudes or every day is a fire drill, select option three and leave. However, only exit after you have found another job, hopefully in a better company.

The first choice "Work within the company to make things better," isn't really a choice. It's a delusion. Unless you are at the senior level of a company, you typically cannot make things better. So, for most people there are only two real choices: make the best of it or leave.

For example, if you have a manager that manages your every move, how can you change that? If he has been at the company for many years, the answer is "you can't." That manager is not going anywhere! Yes, you can build trust with this person, but that doesn't mean his behavior will change. Again, you can change no one except yourself.

"But wait a second," you say. "Aren't there good companies I can work for and enjoy?" Answer: Yes, there are. But the rules for people are the same and all companies contain all types of people. Again, people at work are acquaintances and you must treat them differently than friends. To do otherwise is to leave yourself open and vulnerable.

Summary

- The people you work with are acquaintances. They are not your friends.

- You must treat acquaintances differently. Treat them like customers or clients.

- You can either make the best of a difficult situation or leave. Those are the options for a bad workplace environment.

Questions to Ask Yourself

- Can I work well with the people at my place of employment? If not, why not?

- Do I treat people at work as friends or acquaintances?

- Do I share too much about myself with acquaintances? If so, why?

- Do I understand that the only thing I can control is what I say, what I do and my reaction to others?

Mark A. Baggesen

Organize and Work Methodically

"Productivity is never an accident. It is always the result of a commitment to excellence, intelligent planning, and focused effort."

~ Paul J. Meyer, Author

Planning Done Well

There is an old business axiom: "Plan your work and work your plan." That's the essence of organizing and working methodically. It is an essential part of a drama-free zone. Think about any project in the past that had a positive outcome; more than likely it started with a project plan. Your work should be no different.

Organize

One of the worst feelings you will ever have is not being prepared for work or missing deadlines. That creates lots of drama - potentially for you, your manager and others that depend on you. Were the deadlines unreasonable? Maybe. But maybe you are not organized.

It is easy to do whatever someone tells you to do. That's not really what companies want today. They want people who can think, plan and execute. If you have to be told to do every single step, you may either exhaust your manager, her good will, or both.

Where does that put you? It puts you in control!

It's your job to manage yourself and your work. If you don't manage yourself, your manager will!

Organizing your work is the litmus test that determines if you succeed or fail at the job. No one will look over your shoulder and make you do something. Most companies do not have time for that kind of nonsense.

Organizing your work means arranging it based on priority, complexity, its place in a series and the due date. The more tasks you have, the more planning you will need. It is best to plan on Friday for the next business week. That way, you will know each day what you have to accomplish and you will start

Monday with purpose and direction.

Will your plan change? Probably. But it's easier to change a good plan, than no plan. Here are some ways to evaluate and organize your work queue:

Priority - If you have 5 things to do in one day, some will be more important than others. Assign each task a rating of 1 to 5 with 5 being the most important and 1 being the least important.

Complexity - Define the task as complex or simple and assign an estimated time value (in hours) to complete it.

It's place in a series - Do tasks in a logical order. For example, if you are working on a book, it's good to start with the first chapter, then progress to the second chapter. You don't do "B" before you do "A".

Due Date - Is the deadline 1 day or 1 month? It makes a difference.

After you have identified and valued all tasks, put them in an order that makes sense, and accomplish those during the work week. Whatever you do not complete can either be removed (if not that important), or moved to the following week.

Work Methodically

Working methodically means working the plan you create. Keep track of time and the completion percentage of your tasks. Normally the process works this way:

- The tasks with the highest priority get done first.

- Complexity will tell you how much time you need to work on each task.

- It's place in the series will tell you which of the tasks to do in what order (if applicable).

- Tasks due first, are not completed first. The items due first are only worked on first, if those are the highest priority.

- The lowest priority items (typical 1s or 2s) get done after everything else or those tasks do not get done. The longer the list of tasks you have, the more likely it will be that tasks with a low priority will not get done. There is only so much time in a week.

If your plan does not work this way, negotiate a different timeline for your tasks with your manager.

Summary

- Plan your work. Make adjustments as necessary. Being unorganized will get you nowhere.

- Work your plan. Execute your work well and in a logical order. Not having a good method of work will not help you.

Questions to Ask Yourself

- Do I organize my work?

- Do I plan out a week's work ahead of time? If not, why not?

- When I plan, how often does my work get off track? If often, why is that? What can I do to stay on track?

- Do I work methodically? If so, how has that benefited me? If not, why not?

Time Off or Timeout

"Whenever I'm taking time off, all I'm thinking about is working."

~ Scarlett Johansson, Actress

Take a Break

Work is, for the lack of a better phrase, hard work. If you enjoy it, yes, it can also be your play. However, there is a point when taking a break will do more to rejuvenate your mind and body then continuing to grind through the workday.

Thirty years ago there were 3 people to do one job. Now there is one person to do 3 jobs. The promise that computers would reduce the workload for employees never materialized. That's why you need to treat yourself well and know when taking a break from work is the best thing to do.

It is very typical of today's environment to get caught up in work because there's so much of it! Everyone else seems to be always working. Also, there's all the noise and distraction of digital devices. Here's the problem: it's not healthy and could hurt your productivity, if you're not taking any breaks.

Plan breaks throughout the day. Breaks can be 15 minutes every couple of hours or whatever works best for you. Stand up, stretch, go get something to drink, do something different. Then after you have relaxed your mind and body, return to work. Do your best not to think about work while on break, or you will waste this time off.

Studies have consistently shown that taking breaks make better, more productive employees. Not only are these employees more productive, they are more creative, happier and much less likely to experience burnout.

The lunch break is a great time to network with colleagues, to take a walk, eat lunch and read a book or do something else other than work. It's easy to get caught up in deliverables, timelines and tasks that must get done. However, if you only focus on work, you won't give your mind time to rest. For example, eating lunch at your desk is not a good idea. Take your lunch and eat it somewhere else!

There are many kinds of company philosophies. Some companies don't care what you do as long as the work gets done. Others want their employees to be heads down and just work 8 hours. If you work at your desk all day and don't talk to anyone because you have so much work, you are working in a heads-down environment, whether the company and its managers want to admit it or not. This is not healthy and is a very old-school management philosophy.

Here's a question: If you're working late to impress the boss, but the boss goes home at 5pm, how will he know? The answer is that he will not know. You could always send him an email, but that might disturb his recovery time.

If employers want great employees that are highly competent, creative and collaborative, then encouraging a work-life balance, and positive employee interactions, will go a long way to create that environment. People are not machines or computers. That's why taking breaks to relax the mind and body is so important. Don't expect the company to encourage you to take a timeout, they're too focused on other things. Therefore, you need to create that space for yourself.

Summary

- Take periodic breaks during the workday to be your most productive and healthy.

Questions to Ask Yourself

- Do I take breaks throughout the workday? If not, why?

- Do I feel burned-out at the end of the day? If so, why?

- Do I only think of work when I take a break? If so, how can I change that?

- Do I think anyone will think less of me because I take a short break to refresh my mind?

Mark A. Baggesen

Fear of Missing Out

One of the best ways to deal with the peer pressure of the 'Fear of Missing Out' is to opt-out whenever possible.

~ Dana Perino

FOMO or JOMO?

FOMO is the fear of missing out: Missing out with social media, email, news, text messages, the lottery and just about anything else you can think of that you worry about missing. For example, if you check your email every 5 minutes of the day - even on non-work hours, that's major FOMO. FOMO can drive you crazy, if you let it. Remember, it is your mind - you can control your impulses.

JOMO is the joy of missing out. It's getting rid of all the anxiety, the noise, the worry of missing out. JOMO means enjoying life, the people in front of you and the beautiful day. It frees you from the responsibility of taking part in something that may not give you real joy. JOMO is empowering, where FOMO can be disabling. JOMO is peace, where FOMO can be chaos.

How do you get JOMO? Excellent question, complicated answer. Here is how to start: set limits when you check social media. Make a promise to yourself that you will check it only 3 or 4 times a day like 10am, 2pm, 6pm and 9pm.

Shutoff notifications for all your cell phone applications. You decide when to respond. When you go to bed, shut your phone off and enjoy the bliss of an undisturbed, restful sleep. This won't be easy, but it will be worth it. If you try this for a week, you will undoubtedly experience a new level of joy.

Summary

- FOMO is the Fear of Missing Out
- JOMO is the Joy of Missing Out

Questions to Ask Yourself

- Which of these (FOMO or JOMO) do you current practice?

- Which of these would you prefer to practice in the future?

- What is stopping you from practicing your choice?

Mark A. Baggesen

Computers

"The good news about computers is that they do what you tell them to do. The bad news is that they do what you tell them to do."

~ *Ted Nelson, American I.T. Pioneer & Philosopher*

Technology

Technology is wonderful when it works. It's annoying when it does not. Everyone is an information worker, meaning that they get information from technology or put information into the technology. Regardless of the industry, the profession or the individual job, everyone uses technology. When the unexpected happens with computers and other devices, it stops the flow of information and work.

Without technology (computers, networks, telephones, printers), there is no business environment. Technology is everywhere, all the time and is part of every process and task people do. All modern business processes were first technology processes. It's a fact that you might not realize until "it" does not work.

For example, to do your job you have to start your computer, log into the network, use software and maybe even print something. Every step along the way there are rules for how you have to do things while using the computer. If you use it correctly, it works (most of the time). If you use it incorrectly, it will not give you the result you expect.

It does not matter whether you are talking about Microsoft Windows PCs, Apple MacBooks, Google Chromebooks or Linux machines. All computers, operating systems and applications have rules. Obey their rules and they work (most of the time). Don't obey their rules and you'll get nothing but problems.

Things Made by Man Will Always Break

What happens when you obey the rules and the technology does not work? Drama. Stress. Frustration. Confusion. "Quick someone call desktop support," you hear your mind say.

But wait: Is it still a problem (i.e., there was an error, but now it's gone)? Can you repeat it? If the problem happened only once, count yourself as lucky. You don't need technical support, because the likelihood of figuring out why something happened once is near impossible. Still want to call technical support? OK, fine.

You call desktop support and after a 10 minute queue of music on hold, someone hops on the call and provides 30 minutes of questions. They even offer to "remote in" to your computer and have a look. Depending on your company, you will either get your problem fixed, or you'll be frustrated and not helped. Again, more drama.

What can you do about it? That depends.

Stuff happens. It's just like the saying: "Man is imperfect, man makes computers, therefore computers are imperfect." Yes, I know that's not helpful, but that's the truth.

Are you willing to fix it yourself? Yes? OK, then. There is hope for you.

Power Off (90 Percent Rule)

Did you know that powering off your non-working device, will solve about 90 percent of all problems? Yep, it's true, whether you are talking about a computer, its operating system, a phone, headset, printer, copier or anything else electronic.

Why? The short answer is, well, it just works that way. The longer answer is that sometimes processors, memory, network protocols, and other technical stuff get confused or "hosed" (a perfectly good technical word that means it doesn't work anymore). The quickest way to fix devices is to shut them off for a few minutes, go get a cup of tea, and then turn them back on (the tea is optional).

For example, it used to be that to fix HP printers the user had to shut it off for at least 15 minutes. Why? Because that's how long the printer's memory would keep print job information.

Beyond that time, the memory would be empty. Crazy, right?!

Save Your Work Often

The best way to have no drama from a computer is to save your work. How often? The rule is save whatever you don't want to lose. Many programs have an auto-save feature. You set the time (like 5 minutes) and it will automatically save your work every 5 minutes. Ideally, if you want to lose nothing, press "Ctrl + S" after you type a few lines (on Macs that is "Command + S"). Also, when you start a new file, save it right away, so you can use the save feature without having to think about it much.

Make a Second File Copy

If you keep your work on a cloud drive or network file folder, your work will automatically back up, eventually. When? Again, that depends on how things are set up. If you are not sure, how your computer saves and backs up your work files, ask someone. In the meantime, make a copy of anything you want to protect, in case your original document or device breaks. It doesn't happen often, but it happens. USB drives are handy for storing file copies.

The golden rule for safe computer files: Make sure you make a copy of a file on two different physical devices. Your computer's hard drive is one device, a USB Drive, a network drive or cloud drive is another.

When in Doubt, Read the Directions

Everyone wants to use electronic devices, but no one wants to read the directions. It's understandable, not reasonable, but understandable. (Even technical writers that create user guides, don't enjoy reading them). If you don't read the directions, you won't know the rules to follow. So if you get stuck, just read the manual or the Help file (press F1 on most computers).

The Other 10 Percent

The other 10 percent of technology problems are a mixed bag of troubles: some you can fix, some you cannot. For example, if you're using an MS Windows 10 computer and your wireless network connection goes bad, you can right-click on the network icon (bottom, right taskbar) and select "Troubleshoot Problems." Windows will then go through several processes that may fix it. Likewise, if you have an application that is not working correctly, Windows has a "Repair" feature in the Uninstall Programs section of the Control Panel that may fix the program.

Shutting your computer off and restarting it may also solve these types of problems.

Internet Browsers

Internet Browsers are the only exception to the "power off" or 90 percent rule. This is because sometimes those applications need to have their "cache" and "cookies" deleted. The browser makes a cache or collection of pages and images that you've viewed. Cookies are little tracking mechanisms for advertisers and online applications like Gmail. If your Internet Browser is not working well, it is best to delete these two things, close and restart your browser and see if that fixes your problem.

If You Have a Real Problem That Needs I.T.

Occasionally, computers, hard drives, other equipment and operating systems break and become unserviceable. But it is very rare. When this happens or you can consistently reproduce the error a few times, that's when I.T. can help you fix it. Also, a lot of problems with Internet Browsers, Email and System/Application access often are network related problems that I.T. can fix without looking at your computer.

Summary

- You can fix 90% of all problems with technology by shutting them off.

- Save your work often and have a backup copy of your work on a separate physical device (like a USB drive).

- When in doubt, read the user directions or the help information.

- Often computer operating system utilities can fix problems.

- Once in a great while, there will be a reason to call I.T. support.

Questions to Ask Yourself

- Do I often have problems with computers and other electronic devices? If so, did I try shutting them off?

- Do I save my work often?

- Do I ever read the manuals that come with the equipment I use?

- Do I backup my work to a second physical device?

- Do I call I.T. Support often for things that I can fix?

- Do I call I.T. Support for things they cannot fix (like problems I.T. cannot reproduced)?

Honesty vs. Lies

"I've always operated under the notion that audiences don't always know when they're being lied to, but that they always know when they're being told the truth."

~ Sean Penn, Actor

Lies

Lies complicate everything. Only a consummate liar can remember the difference between the truth and his lies until eventually all those become the same: a dirty lie.

Lies create drama, lots of it (that's why they are dirty). Lies require more thought, organization and energy to remember correctly. Eventually, all liars are caught in a lie-it's just a matter of time.

According to a 2002 survey by a researcher at the University of Massachusetts/Amherst, in any 10 minute conversation at work 60% of people lie at least once. Most lie 2 or 3 times.

Lying is an epidemic, and it will not get better soon. The more people lie, the more they believe their own lies. At some point even they cannot tell the difference between the truth and the lie. That's why job recruiters don't believe honest candidates-because most people pad their resumes to the point there's not much truth in it. Think this is incorrect? Consider this: In 2017, according to HireRight (an American background screening company) 85 percent of employers caught applicants lying on their resumes.

Here are some reasons that people lie:

They lie to protect themselves - from something they said previously or bad behaviors.

They lie to harm others - There are vindictive people in the workplace that jockey to promote themselves, to harm others, to manipulate others and to "get even" whatever that means. This has always been an element of society. Knowing this is an element in every workplace is important.

They lie to feel superior - Like the analogy of the short man that puts 2 inch lifts into his shoes to look taller or raises his chair higher than everyone else at the table, people lie like rugs to make themselves out to be better, smarter, or more successful. They lie about their status, accomplishments, work history, education, you name it. It would not be accurate to say that only losers lie, because 60% of everyone is lying all the time.

They lie to procrastinate or avoid something - If they don't want to do something, they just lie about it. "Oh, sorry I didn't have time...", or "Yes, I did it why?" Like the small child that learns to say yes to anything his parents ask, then he does whatever he wants. Lying is an easy way for people to cover their actions or inaction.

In Public Relations (PR) the first thing they will teach you, when being approached by a news reporter, is to ask "What is the story?" This is because the story could be about anything and in PR you don't want to give reporters too much information. The reporter already knows the story before they knock on your door.

The second thing in PR they will teach you is to "answer the question you want to answer." This means, regardless of the question asked, answer the question with what you want to say (regardless if it answers their question)." This is why almost no politician or lawyer ever gives a direct answer.

Know that liars are everywhere, all the time. I know it's not a positive thing to say, but it is unfortunately true. If you have spoken to several people at work today, then you have already been lied to at least twice.

Honesty

This section will be short. Why? Honesty does not require much heavy lifting.

Does honesty always work? Usually, unless it is something negative. The adage "if you have nothing good to say, say nothing" is correct. If you can't tell the truth at work, avoid the subject when possible.

But "wait a second," you say. "Isn't avoiding the subject the same as lying?" The answer is no, it's not lying. It's called being careful. If you say something bad about someone or something, it may harm you for years in that workplace and possibly beyond.

One of the most valuable commodities in life is trust. Trust is very difficult to earn because so many people lie. It really is unbelievable. Lies destroy trust and once trust is lost, it is gone forever, because how can you trust someone who has already lied to your face once?

So, if you want to avoid drama, be honest.

Summary

- Lies create drama. If you tell the truth, you have nothing to worry about and no drama.

Questions to Ask Yourself

- Has someone ever caught me lying? What was the result? How did I feel?

- Do I ever tell "white lies?" If yes, do I really think that's not a lie?

- Have I ever caught someone else lying to me? What did I do and how did I feel?

Chapter 2:
Create a Drama-Free Zone For Peers

"Success is not two cars or a swimming pool. It's the approval of your peers."

~ Peter Finch, Actor

It's Only Human

Everything in this world is human relationships. This is especially true in the workplace. How you get along and work with others will determine more about your success than anything else in your career. You can be the smartest, best manager or individual contributor in the world, but if the people at work don't like or respect you, you will not develop much of a professional network (that will help you when you need it) and your career will suffer.

This section talks about what you can do to improve your relationship with peers and in the process build that drama-free zone with them.

Treat Everyone as an Individual and Equal

There's a lot of buzz in the news about treating everyone with respect and acceptance. Yes, you can do that, but that alone is not enough. If you really want to develop solid relationships in the workplace, treat people well and treat each person as an individual (as they want to be treated).

Everyone in the world is different. As Lewis Black says "We are all snowflakes." Each has unique likes and dislikes, mannerisms, skill sets, interests, personalities and challenges. You should understand those differences if you want to deepen any relationship, business or personal. The only way to build relationships with others is by interacting with them in a way that's good for them. Dale Carnegie said "speak to people in terms of their point of view." That's exactly the point.

Equal. What does that mean? Everyone is not equal-that's the truth. However, people should treat others equally and fairly in the workplace. No one is better than another. Some are richer, some are smarter, some have different skill sets, but everyone is equal and deserves respect.

Set Up Relationships for Success

The first step to setting up a relationship for success is to learn about the person you would like to develop a working relationship with. Why? Because otherwise you will not understand who you are talking to and you might say the wrong thing to the wrong person.

There are many ways to research people. Here are a few: googling them, looking at their LinkedIn profile and asking other people. Social media is awash with information about people (probably more than you will want to know).

The important thing is to have a point of reference (if possible) before you speak with them. For example, if you can find out someone's job history and the things they have done, any hobbies and their likes and dislikes, you will have a lot of information that can be helpful in understanding them. Some people may think it is "creepy" to google someone else-but everyone does it. If you research someone for a good purpose, it means that you care about them.

Often people just work with strangers because they do not take the time to create that relationship. You need to decide if you want to work with strangers or acquaintances and colleagues with whom you have some bond. Stephen Covey calls this "deposits in the emotional bank account." In other words, if you have a solid working relationship with people at the office, it will be because you have invested your time and your effort to develop that relationship.

Ask the Right Questions

Questions are magical things. Questions can open up a world like nothing else. In the workplace, the right questions will give you keen insight into others, events and anything else you want to know.

Ask people open questions about their experiences, likes and dislike and what projects they are working on currently. If they ask you questions, share some of yourself with them. That's how you build a bond. No one lives in a vacuum, you will probably find things in common with the other person-it's just human nature.

Daily Acknowledgment

It may sound unimportant but saying hello and goodbye at the beginning and end of the day acknowledges the other person's existence and presence. No one likes to be ignored or taken for granted. If you treat people that way, they will be just as indifferent to you. Yes, acknowledging people is civility and good manners, but it's also common sense and very important.

Think about the last time you were working, and no one said anything to you all day-unless they needed something. How did that make you feel?

Gossip

The rumor mill is everywhere in companies and has always been a factor in the workplace. Sometimes the rumors are correct, sometimes not. Rumor is just another word for gossip. Gossip is a negative, destructive activity that too many people take part in because they don't know any better.

When you hear a rumor or gossip about another person, let it end with you. Don't spread it to the next person. You are not a chain letter. It's OK to listen to the rumor mill, if you have to, but avoid taking part in it. Being a participant will only cause you harm long term and those around you will trust you less. Why? Look at it this way: if you say something negative about another employee, the person next to you may wonder "what does he say about me when I am not around?"

Don't take part in the rumor mill. It's not a good way to learn the truth about anything and in the long term it could hurt you.

Participating in gossip will only increase the potential of drama in the workspace.

Thinking vs. Speaking

Speaking is not thinking. Some people equate one with the other, but speaking is not thinking and it never will be. That's why it is important that you first think about what it is you want to say before you say it. Don't speak "off the top of your head" or just say the first thing that comes into your mind. You will only regret it.

You may think the idea that thinking does not equal speaking is absurd or obvious, but it's not - at least not for many people. Talking without thinking is OK if you're by yourself and maybe if you're outside of work with friends, but you still may regret it.

How many people do you know that do this? Think a moment about any public person who you disagree with, or that is constantly getting into problems for what they say. Next, think about what they said. Do you see a correlation between the lack of thinking and speaking?

No? Ok. Think of a politician you think says idiotic things. That should be easy enough. Do you really think what they said is something they thought about before they said it? Perhaps not.

Every time someone, anyone says something stupid or rude, the chances are high that they did not think about what they would say before they said it. Otherwise, they would not have said it or they would have said something else.

Your mouth is your own. Use it as you wish. Hopefully, you'll think about what you will say before you put words in it.

Think first, pause, then speak.

Judging Others

Judging others is a dangerous practice. An old saying states "judge not, lest ye not be judged." Despite that, elders teach us to judge people, options, opportunities and situations.

If you judge others, you put yourself in a position that can feel higher or better than the other person. The problem with that is that it's not real or true. All people are at the same level. No one enjoys being judged, not even the CEO of your company.

If you judge people harshly, it will almost always backfire, harm you and create drama. That's why it's such a dangerous practice.

Life, even for the most gregarious, is a voyage of one. We each pass this life and eventual death on our own. Judging others is deceptive because often we do not understand what other people are going through in their lives. Most of the time, if you judge people, you will be wrong.

The person next to you might have a relative dying of cancer, be going through a divorce, have an elderly parent they are taking care of, have crushing debt from college loans that is causing bankruptcy or a child that is mentally ill. The truth is no one knows what other people are going through in this world. So give yourself and everyone else the benefit of the doubt. We're only human.

Worse than judging others is saying what you think, based on that judgment. That is the easiest way to get into trouble in the workplace or anywhere else. It is better to understand others and have some compassion and empathy for those we don't know - that creates a drama-free zone.

Divisive Topics

Divisive subjects are difficult and dangerous in the

workplace. Here's a little insight: No one knows what you are thinking about until you say something or make an expression on your face. Knowing this should insulate you from worrying about topics that are controversial. Few things cause drama as easily as divisive topics.

It seems like in today's world almost every social topic or controversy is acceptable and defended. That makes it very difficult to express one's opinion if there is disagreement. In the workplace or with people you work with, the best way is to avoid talking about all these issues, whether it's Politics, Religion, Race, Gender Identification or anything else that's a hot button topic. Doing this won't make you weak, it will make you smart and easier to work with. There will be less drama.

The workplace is for work. If you want to have a discussion about anything other than work, do that in your private life, not in the office. What you need to understand is that no one in the workplace wants to hear what you have to say about social issues, especially if you disagree with them.

If someone tries to talk with you about social issues of any kind, either don't respond (that's usually best) or if they push you for a response just say "thanks, but I don't talk about those things at work." Next, change the subject. If you can say that with a considerate or kind tone in your voice and no expression on your face that's even better.

The people that do best in corporate and company climates are the ones that are savvy enough to leave their opinions on things not work-related, outside of work.

People You Work With (Co-Workers)

Companies used to never allow employees to date other employees (coworkers) from the same workplace. Now with company policies changing some are allowing this practice, provided that there's no manager-employee relationship between the two people.

The best idea regarding dating someone you work with: Don't do it! Never! Not under any circumstances! (If it looks like I am shouting here, it is because I am). This is one of the easiest ways to destroy a drama-free zone, because dating is all emotion.

There's the reason people say it's a bad idea. Because it is a bad idea.

For example, if you date someone that lives in the apartment next to yours, where can you go if the relationship doesn't work out? You can't go home, that's where the other person lives!

It's understandable that you work very hard and long hours and have little time to find someone to date outside of work. But there are dozens of ways to meet others. You can meet people through friends and family, through your church, at the market, stores or at the gym. You can meet people anywhere and everywhere (if you just get off that mobile phone or PC and leave your home. There are even online dating sites for people that cannot unplug). Don't look at work for people to date, it's a bad idea.

Like any other decision you make in life or business, first consider the consequences before you do something. If dating someone you work with doesn't work out, what's the worst that can happen? Not only can it blow up your work relationship and make the workplace difficult, it can also bring unnecessary drama into an otherwise amiable office. And it might cause you or the other person to leave the company. Is that what you really want?

So, it's not that you can't date a co-worker; it's that you should not. Most people want to do a good day's work (and get paid for it), go home and leave their company in the rearview mirror. They don't go to work for any other reason.

Empathy

Empathy is the ability to understand and share the feelings of another person. It's the ability to put yourself in someone else's position and understand what they experience.

Empathy is among the best skills of humanity. Only humans can feel empathy.

If someone is having difficulty with something or someone, the most considerate thing you can do is to listen and be a sounding board for this person. If there's something you can do to help, you can offer that-it's up to you. Just know this: you can't help people that don't want your help.

The opposite of empathy is schadenfreude, a German word that translated literally means "damage joy." It is the happiness derived from someone else's misfortune. For example, if Bob is not a nice person, then he loses his job, you are happy about that.

Schadenfreude is akin to "dancing on someone's grave." It's just something that civil people do not do because it is disrespectful and it will lessen you as a human being. Also, people around you will recognize that as a shortcoming in your character, so never share that feeling with anyone.

Empathy will help create that drama-free zone for you and your peers.

How You Dress

This is the rule: Don't dress in a way that makes other people uncomfortable.

Dressing for work shouldn't be difficult. Clothing should always be conservative for both men and women. You know what that means: ironed shirts and pants for men, the same or dresses for women, showing no cleavage or no skirts above the knees.

If you want to create a drama-free zone, avoid wearing clothing that makes other people uncomfortable: this means do not wear leotards or body hose, sweat pants or shirts, shirts half opened, skirts that are too short, t-shirts, shorts, flip-flops or anything else that you would wear around the house. It seems like in today's office environment anything and everything goes - no matter how inappropriate. So you can wear whatever you want at the office, just know that people always will judge you according to what you wear at work. If it makes someone uncomfortable, you have just introduced drama into the workplace.

How you dress says a lot about who you are and who you want to be. How you dress at work should be nothing other than professional. Dressing well will also help your career.

Dress properly for work and contribute to creating that drama-free zone.

Bad Language

Using profanity or foul language is the fastest way to create drama in the workplace. Don't do it. It is never acceptable in any language nor any professional situation. Language is a powerful tool for success or a liability that will cause you problems.

Also, if you and a friend speak any language other than English, always speak English in the workplace around other people. It is annoying and impolite to speak another language around people that don't speak your language. It may not be fair and you may talk innocently about nothing, but that will not be the perception.

Whatever is the language of the business (yes, companies designate that), should be the language you speak. Never use profanity or foul words in the workplace or in social situations with people from work.

Summary

- Everything in this world is human relationships.
- Treat everyone well and as an individual. Treat everyone as your equal.
- Learn about people in the workplace before you engage them in conversation.
- Ask people open questions.
- Acknowledge people when you arrive and leave work.
- Avoid the gossip and rumor mill.
- Think first, then a pause, then speak.
- Avoid judging others.
- Don't talk about divisive subjects at work.
- Don't date people from work.
- Treat everyone with empathy.
- Dress so you don't make others feel uncomfortable.
- Never use profanity or foul language in the workplace

Questions to Ask Yourself

- Do I treat people as individuals?
- Do I treat people equally? If not, why?
- Do I know something about the people I talk with or do I just talk with anyone without knowing anything about them?
- Do I ask people the right questions?
- Do I acknowledge people when arriving at and leaving work?
- Do I participate in gossip? If so why? What is that gaining

you?

- Do I judge people? If so, do I really know much about them?

- Do I talk about inappropriate subjects at work? Like politics, religion, social issues? If so, why?

- Do I try to date co-workers? If so, how has that worked out for me? Have there ever been negative consequences?

- Do I understand what empathy is?

- Do I have empathy for others? If not, why not?

- Do I dress appropriately for the workplace? If not, why?

- Do I do or say things that make other people uncomfortable? If so, why? How is the benefiting me?

- Do I use profanity or bad language at work? If so, why?

Chapter 3:
Create a Drama-Free Zone for Your Manager

"The players make the manager, it's never the other way."

~ Sparky Anderson, American Major League Player, Coach, and Manager

Why Create a Drama-Free Zone for Managers?

Consider the experience of traveling by plane: There is packing your bags, getting ready for the trip, getting to the airport, checking in bags, worry about others (if you have kids with you), getting your boarding pass, getting through the TSA checkpoint, walking to the gate, waiting, walking to another gate (if the gate changed), watching out for strangers and thieves, boarding the plane and arranging your carry-on bags. Then you sit down. Do you remember the relief you felt when you finally sat down on the plane after all that effort?

A manager's day is like traveling by plane every day. There are dozens of things to worry about and many complex steps. Only when the day is over can managers relax and rest (and that's only if they shut off their phone and PC). Unless you create a drama-free zone. Then your manager can relax at least sometimes.

Managers often consider the job of management as both "the best of all worlds" and "proof that no good deed goes unpunished." This is because people often act like children in kindergarten. There is whining, arguments, people missing deadlines, people upsetting clients, absences without cause, those employees taking 2-hour lunches, those missing key meetings, sub-quality work product, etc., etc., etc.

Create a drama-free zone means you are the adult in the room. It means your behavior is the same every day–no whining, no surprises, no issues, no problems, no drama. Your meeting with your manager may be the only easy, drama-free meeting they have all week. You become for them an ally they can trust; one less person they have to worry about.

These are the steps to create this drama-free zone:

- Manage your manager

- No surprises
- Set achievable expectations
- Warn them as soon as you can
- Make it easy for them
- Do what you say you will do
- Be reliable and trustworthy
- Always make them look good
- With a problem have solutions

Manage Your Manager

Do you think your manager must manage you? Think again. Is that really the best use of his or her time?

Everyone should manage the relationship they have with their manager. But many people just plod through work, without giving it a second thought. Managing your manager is essential to having an excellent relationship, establishing trust and building your career. Consider this: if you don't manage your manager, they will have to manage you. Which way would you rather have it?

No Surprises

No one likes surprises, but managers because of their occupation really HATE surprises. Surprises = DRAMA. All managers have so many things to think about very day, the last thing they want or need is for one of their employees to drop a big "SURPRISE!" bomb on their desk.

A "SURPRISE" bomb may literally blow up your manager's day. It will be one more unexpected thing they have to deal with because you didn't or couldn't handle it. Is that something you really want to happen? How do you think your manager will react?

A drama-free zone for a manager, means no employee surprises.

Set Achievable Expectations

You must negotiate with your manager realistic, achievable goals and deadlines for projects and deliverables. Otherwise, this will create drama. Setting achievable expectations is an essential part of managing your manager. If you need more time, don't wait until the last day to ask for another 2 weeks. Ask for more time at the beginning of the project. Managers are adults - they can handle the truth, so say it!

Not setting achievable expectations with your manager is one of the best ways to create drama. Worse yet, they will trust you less and likely feel the need to watch over your work more closely.

If you set achievable expectations and accomplish those, how do you think your manager will feel about you?

A drama-free zone for a manager, means employees meeting their responsibilities.

Warn Them as Soon as You Can

When you see trouble coming, let your management know!

You have intuition, so you know when something doesn't seem right. It could be your little voice saying "I don't think this vendor will meet their deadline," it could be "at this rate I will use up the annual advertising budget in only 6 months." The point is, there are always signs before something goes wrong; whether that's 3 months or 3 days from now. Your job is to recognize those signs and do something about it!

You must warn your manager when you think anything negative could happen – this isn't "crying wolf." This is "raising the flag" and saying "we need to look at this to discern the risk, it's effect on the project and to put into place preventative measures." Also, it gives the manager time to think – you're not telling them at the last moment, so there's time to come up with a well thought out mitigation plan.

Such a conversation is also an opportunity to discuss fully the situation and develop trust. Your manager will know that you are warning them to protect them from a failure somewhere and they will appreciate it.

Make it Easy for Them

Make interactions with your manager something pleasant and predictable so he can relax when he talks with you. For example, If you have a meeting with him and you want to talk about an email or several emails you sent him in the past week, have those emails printed out and with you for the meeting. Don't expect he will remember your email or know where it is.

Do What You Say You Will Do

Do what you say you will do. When you make a commitment with your manager, honor that commitment. If you say you will be in at 7 A.M. on Saturday to get the packages ready for 10 A.M. shipment to a trade show next Monday, you had better be there at 7 A.M. Showing up at 8 A.M. won't earn you any trust points. Especially, if you find that your manager came in and finished your work.

If you aren't acting and building this kind of trust and expectations with your manager, eventually you may regret it.

Be Reliable and Trustworthy

Nothing says you like and respect your manager as much as being reliable and trustworthy and doing that consistently over a proven period. That is the gold standard everyone should work towards. If you aren't doing that, reconsider whether you really want to do that job.

The alternative to being reliable and trustworthy is that you become a liability or a negative variable for the manager. Liabilities and variables are mitigated or removed.

A drama-free zone for a manager means employees that are reliable and trustworthy.

Always Make Them Look Good

Always strive to make your manager look good. They can't be everywhere all the time and you are their representative when they aren't there. If you think you only represent yourself anytime you do something, think again. You work for someone and that person is accountable for you. If you do something wrong, they get the call, not you. They become the one that has to handle "something."

When you don't see your manager, it is because she is earnestly working on something–she may even hide out in a different part of the building to get work done. There is no other reason managers are absent from view.

If your manager creates a project for you to do and it turns out well, give them their due credit for their role in the project- praise them directly. They never get that kind of praise from employees, they will appreciate it. Just to clarify, I am not talking about brown-nosing. I am talking about only sincere, deserved praise.

You may find this shocking, but managers are only people– just like you and me. Managers are far from perfect. Occasionally they will forget things, fail at something, remember something incorrectly. When this happens, don't be the one that sits silent or puts them on the spot. Be the person who asks this question "What can I do to help you resolve this?" Managers can and will fall short, like everyone else.

The last time you fell short of a goal, what did your manager do or say to you?

With Problems Have Solutions

When you go to your manager with a problem or roadblock, have a list of solutions. Don't expect that your manager will just solve it for you. Only children expect their parents to make everything all right.

Managers need problem solvers, because the world and work are full of problems. While one of their jobs is to "remove roadblocks" from your path, it isn't true they have to figure out the best solution. You are the subject expert of whatever is going on. Your manager may know nothing about it.

Once you have identified a problem that requires your manager's input or help, spend time to develop different scenarios that can solve the problem. Chart out on paper or slides the problem and solutions. Then go to your manager and say "I have a problem that needs your review and input. Would you be able to look at what I have prepared and give me feedback on solutions?" It will thrill your manager to do this because again, most people won't bother.

Summary

There are rules for managing your manager. These include:

- Never surprise your manager.
- Always warn them when you see trouble coming.
- Negotiate fair and achievable expectations.
- Build trust.
- Be the adult in the room, not the child.
- Always make your manager look good.

- When you have a problem, go to them with solutions.

Questions to Ask Yourself

- The last time I surprised a manager, what was his or her reaction? What were the consequences for me?

- Have I seen trouble coming in the past and not recognized it? If so why? What was the outcome afterward?

- Do I work in a drama-free zone or do I create a drama zone? If I create drama why? What do I get out of it? Is my work life better or worse for it?

- Am I the child or the adult in the room? If I am the child why? What do I get out of being the child?

- The last time I went to a manager with a problem, did I also bring solutions? If not, why not? Did I think he or she should solve all my problems? What was the result? How did I feel afterward?

Chapter 4:
Create a Drama-Free Zone for Your Employees

"The No. 1 reason people quit their jobs is a bad boss or immediate supervisor."

~ Gallop Poll, 2017

Your Employees

In the 1943 play "No Exit", Sartre says "Hell is other people." For employees in the workplace, hell is a bad or poorly trained manager.

Often when companies promote individual contributors to management, they do so with no training or guidance. This is unfortunate, but it happens all the time. The higher up's rationale is "Bob is a great individual contributor, so he ought to be a great manager too." Unfortunately, this is not true without management training because the skill sets of an individual contributor and manager are very different. Anyone can be an individual contributor but not everyone can be a manager. Becoming a good manager requires study, work and reflection. This situation also applies to people promoted to "Supervisor."

It is because of inept management that experts say employees quit managers, not companies. Whether your employees will quit you, depends on how you treat them. The good news is that you can train most people to be effective and successful managers. It is a learned skill. Good managers are not born they are made.

One of the easiest ways to make employees stay is to create a drama-free zone. It is an invisible barrier that marks the perimeter of your employees' workplace, whether that is physical or virtual. A drama-free zone is an area of trust where all are safe from "outside destructive forces" or anything else unpleasant.

This is not a book on Management or Servant Leadership. If you want to read one of those books, there are many available. This section talks specifically about what you can do now to improve the daily work life of your employees.

Build Trust

Every relationship that has ever succeeded, has done so because of trust. There is no substitute for trust in any relationship nor in any environment.

Trust must go both ways. It is not enough that you trust your employees. Your employees must trust you. If there is an imbalance on either side, that means problems and drama.

Every manager must have the trust of her employees. Otherwise, she is doomed to failure, because it is employees that make managers successful. It is the employees that make up most of the company and do the lion's share of the work. A manager without great employees is like a king of nothing or an emperor with no clothes.

Above all else, you must create an environment of trust.

Be Predictable and Consistent

One attribute employees like is consistency; another is predictability.

If you want to be a manager that creates and maintains a drama-free zone for his or her employees, you must exemplify these qualities.

Every day, make it a point to act the same. You should treat people the same. Even if you're having a bad day, your demeanor needs to be the same as the day before. Do that and your employees will know that any day they need something from you, they don't have to worry if you are having a "bad day" or are "not to be bothered."

When employees know they can depend on their manager any day of the week, that is the beginning of a solid relationship based on trust and a minimum of drama.

Understand Them

To manage employees successfully, you must understand them well. Otherwise, you will make painful mistakes and wrong decisions.

One place to start on a new job is to have a half hour "get to know you" meeting with each employee. Get a copy of their resume before the meeting and study it. Make notes and questions. Read their previous annual management and performance reviews. If you prepare, you will be ready for a great meeting and understand each employee.

During the meeting ask them about their likes and dislikes, dreams for their career and the current dynamics of the organization. The more good questions you ask, the better you will understand them and the current work culture.

Use all that great knowledge when you manage those employees and navigate the work environment.

SWOT Ranking

Everyone has strengths and weaknesses. It is important to understand what those are for each of your people. Also, you must learn their opportunities (what they could be good at doing) and threats (what could cause them to fail at something). These four things make the SWOT ranking.

SWOT analysis (or matrix) is used for business strategic planning. It identifies the strengths, weaknesses, opportunities, and threats related to achieving a specific project, business initiative or analyzing market competition. A SWOT analysis for people is very insightful. It is one good way to understand your people, their skills, what they are interested in doing and what is holding them back from thriving in the workplace.

The manager's job is to assure that their employees are in the right job and performing well for themselves, your organization and the company. Happy employees are ones challenged and that enjoy their work. It is the best way to match their interests with their abilities. When these are mismatched, problems can occur in the workplace.

For example, say you have a person who was a Math major in college. You find (when you become their manager) that they are in a customer service job and performing poorly. Is it really any wonder that this person is unhappy? They are a numbers monster, not a salesperson. Do you see the mismatch?

If you have a SWOT profile for each of your employees, it will be useful for evaluating business needs and areas of employee development. Long term, this profile will help you strengthen the organization and employee skill sets. All employees want to progress beyond their current role and duties. Understanding their SWOT profile is one more piece of the puzzle.

Delegate Well

Managers that are effective learn to delegate well. The ability to delegate is paramount to the success of both the manager and the employee. This is how great managers multiple themselves through others.

Delegation is simple: Give an employee a task, along with the time and tools to be successful, then leave them alone to complete their work. While you are building trust, inspection their progress periodically (depending on the time) during the project.

When the project is complete, give them feedback (both positive and constructive). That's how a manager and an employee will learn what they require, what each expects and how to align their understanding to what success and "done" means (in terms of quality).

The more tasks you delegate to a successful employee the less you will need to inspect their work. This enables the employee to be creative and independent and allows the manager to focus on other important tasks and projects.

Do these delegation steps with each employee. It will quickly become clear, which employees need more coaching and training. Based on that knowledge, give these people the remedial training they need to be successful and again delegate and measure outcomes.

Set achievable goals and deadlines

Goals without deadlines are nothing. Deadlines and goals must be achievable and challenging for the employee. This is where management sometime makes mistakes.

Setting goals for employees is essential. Employees must know what they need to focus on for work. Goals should also challenge, meaning that those should stretch and grow the employee. The bar should always be a little higher than the previous time.

Deadlines are essential so that managers define when work must be completed to meet business expectations. However, deadlines need to be determined based on realistic estimates of the work. The manager and employee should negotiate these estimates so there is mutual agreement. If a manager only dictates when he wants something done, it may not be achievable because of other projects or the complexity of the desired goal.

Deadlines and goals should be reasonable, best estimates. That's the only way the manager and the employee will be successful. Without this understanding and agreement, quality and timelines may suffer.

No Micromanagement

"Nearly all men can stand adversity, but if you want to test a man's character, give him power." - Abraham Lincoln

Of all the things you can do wrong as a manager, micromanaging your employees is among the worst. This action will always create huge drama and very unhappy people.

Micromanaged employees have no real way of becoming successful because every decision is made for them by someone else. It is as if they are a child constantly vulnerable to the whims of a helicopter parent.

Anyone managed this way knows what I am talking about. For those of you that have never experienced this, I will relate a story of what true micromanagement can do to you, your peers and the company you work for.

This is a short story of how micromanagement has played a part in my career.

They recruited me to start at a company in a director position. The company even moved me across the country for this opportunity. I was very excited about this role and had just finished a stellar year where projects I managed exceeded all expectation of the stakeholders, the organization and my VP.

After I started the new job, I noticed that my new manager trusted nothing that I did and objected to almost everything that I accomplished. Conversations with him didn't help clarify anything for me. I was so micromanaged that I could not even have a meeting with another department without him there in the same room. Think about it: If you are hired to lead an organization, and no one lets you lead it, why even be there?

All I could do was protect my people, grow the organization and mission as well as possible and duck anytime he was around. I left the company after 14 months. The experience truly sucked the life out of me to the point I never wanted to have a senior management position again.

Later, I found out that this manager, who had been at the company for 20-plus years, had gone through 11 Marketing

Directors in 10 years, 4 Web Directors in 2 years and countless other people in his 20 years as management. Eventually this manager, and others who protected him in the organization were fired. Still, the damage was done both to the individuals and the company.

Here's the irony: He was a very smart person; some might say brilliant. His problem was that he could not delegate, nor manage those under him and because of that everyone suffered, including him and the company. He trusted no one, and no one trusted him (not even those that protected him). Everyone lost something, and it was all unnecessary.

So, if you want to manage people, learn how to delegate, build trust and that drama-free zone. Take several years to study, learn and reflect on the best management practices available. Otherwise, you may not be equipped to manage anyone.

If you have experienced a micromanager, please share your story, including the resulting impact to your career, with me. I may write a book on micromanagement, if enough people share their stories. I will never publish anything without your permission. This practice has to stop!

Give Them Credit for Their Accomplishments

When others recognize one's work, it is important that you give credit to the person who did the work or created a concept that solved a problem. Yes, ultimately management is responsible for employee deliverables, but that doesn't mean they get to take credit for other people's work. Would you want to work for someone that always took credit for the things you accomplished?

Helping Others

As a manager, your responsibility is to make sure employees

have the tools and the skills to be successful. Despite that help, employees sometimes fail in their job or tasks. In that case, ask them if they need or want help. If they do, help them. If they do not, leave them alone.

Not everyone will ask for or even want your help. This is not only true of specific tasks but also their career. You may see that an employee is making a mistake or "going down the wrong path", but maybe they need to do that to learn a hard lesson.

No one can help someone that does not want help.

Personal Life

If something is not right at home, work will always suffer. As a manager, you're not responsible for your employees' personal life. But when you see an employee that is going through a personal crisis, it is helpful to ask questions and assure they understand the resources available to them (as part of employee benefits, often companies have programs for people that need counseling). At the very least you can empathize with them.

For example, being a sounding board for an employee that is going through a crisis may be the only opportunity that they have to speak with someone about it. Be sure to never judge them nor divulge to others what they say in private.

Life happens to everyone. Being a manager that is empathetic and supportive will help employees when necessary.

One Hour of Training Each Day

As a manager, another great thing you can do for employees is make sure their skills and talents are always growing and current. One way to do that is by scheduling work so that each employee can spend one hour a day on professional development. There are literally millions of classes online. Many companies have internal "universities" or relationships with training companies that offer all kinds of education to employees for no cost.

Besides formal education, professional certifications can help employees build a career. Some certifications are almost mandatory these days.

It's not your job to choose the classes they take. It is your responsibility to make sure they have the time each day to pursue continuous learning. The coursework they study should be in line with their career development plan identified each year at the annual employee review. Also, taking this time to cross-train employees in other jobs of the organization is a great way to strengthen employee skills and to build depth in the organization.

If you had one hour a day to learn something new, how would it benefit you? What would you do with that hour?

Career Planning

As a manager, have you ever asked an employee "Where to you want to be in 5 or 10 years in your career?"

Career planning removes the randomness of career success and focuses the individual on achievable goals. As a manager, if you really want to be doing the right thing for each of your employees, you need to ask these questions.

There's an old saying "if you don't know where you want to be in 10 years, you will be somewhere (just not where you expect)." This does not have to be the case for your employees, but it takes planning and thought to craft a career plan. Otherwise, their career path may be as certain as winning the lottery.

Everyone should have a career plan. Career planning is an important part of management's role.

What Employees Hate

The following is a list of things that employees hate about their managers. This is not an exhaustive list.

Employees hate managers that:

- take credit for their work or ideas
- micromanage
- berate or belittle them
- don't give them space, time and tools to be successful
- have unrealistic expectations
- are never available
- call them at all hours and weekends
- don't support them
- are incompetent
- show favoritism
- can't show employees a career progression and opportunities
- over-communicate
- can't run an effective meeting
- can't make sure employees are fairly paid
- are always late to meetings
- "Hit on" employees

Any of the previously named things should not need further explanation. All can cause serious drama in the workplace.

Summary

- Learn how to be a well-trained manager.

- Build trust with your employees.

- Learn all about employee capabilities, goals and needs.

- Set achievable goals and deadlines.

- Avoid being a micromanager.

- Recognize employees for their good works and ideas.

- Help only those people that want help.

- For employees going through a personal crisis, make sure they know what help is available to them via their employee benefits and other company programs.

- Schedule employees work to include one hour of study a day.

- Avoid anything employees hate that's listed above.

Questions to Ask Yourself

- Have I done the right training and study to be a good manager? In what areas could I improve?

- Do my employees trust me? If not, why? What can I do to remedy that?

- Do I trust my employees? If not, why? What can I do to remedy that?

- Do I understand my employees? Have I done a SWOT profile on them?

- Do I set goals and deadlines that people can meet? Have employees missed these in the past? If so, why?

- Do I feel the need to micromanage anyone that works for me? If so, why? What would be a better technique to get positive results from this person?

- Do I give credit to my employees for their work and ideas? Do I celebrate their wins?

- How well do I handle people that have personal problems? What can I do better?

- Are the skills of all employees current? If not, why not?

- Do I schedule one study hour a day for each employee?

- Have I done career planning with each employee? If not, why not? What resources are available to me to get them started?

Mark A. Baggesen

Don't Work Stupid, Coach Yourself

Here is a sample from my bestselling first book "Don't Work Stupid, Coach Yourself." It's for anyone that wants more out of life and is willing to ask the hard questions to get it.

Enjoy.

Chapter 1: Where Have You Been?

This chapter requires you to be brutally honest with yourself. It is important to take stock in what you have done and where you have been in the past. For each question, take a few minutes to think about the answer and write it down.

Questions to Ask Yourself

Start by asking yourself these questions:

- Am I now where I thought I would be 5 or 10 years ago?

- Am I where I wanted to be in my career and life?

If the answer is yes: Outstanding! Congratulations!

If the answer is no, that's okay. But it's important to look at this. Ask yourself the following questions and write the answers:

- What did I want to be 5 or 10 years ago?

- What did I try to achieve that?

- Did I have a cohesive, well thought out plan? If, yes, what kept me from fulfilling that plan?

- Do I have any regrets about where I am in my life and career today?

- What would I do differently if I had the chance for a do-over?

The Past is the Past

The previous questions may evoke strong emotions in you. This is good! The purpose of this exercise isn't to "beat yourself up." The purpose is to give you insight into how fast life moves and that time waits for no one. That said, the past is the past and we can't do anything about it–it's done, finished, unchangeable, kaput, over. So, let it go. Your future will be fantastic!

Make a commitment to yourself right now. Commit 100% to making the next 10 years, a world of YOUR MAKING.

You can achieve all you want in your life and career. Begin by understanding that every day is a gift, and it is your decision how you use it. You can use it with purpose, or you can waste it and just let things happen. Once the day is over, it's over.

Commit to Yourself

Write this commitment statement (or one like it) on a blank piece of paper, sign and date it or use the free worksheet from the website.

Today, I totally commit to making the next 10 years, a future of MY MAKING.

I can do ANYTHING–I know that now.

I will use every day as if it were my last.

I understand that every new day is one more day than given to someone else.

I will create a plan for my future.

I will follow that plan so in 10 years, I will be where I want to be.

I will create my destiny!

Signed, <your name>   Today's Date is:

Put your signed statement on a wall or refrigerator–anywhere you will see it every day.

Summary

- The past is the past, leave it there. This is your time. Use each day to its maximum.

Questions to Ask Yourself

- Have I taken the time to honestly and fully answer this chapter's questions?

- Am I able to let go of the past and move forward? If not, why not?

- Is there anything else that's now holding me back? If yes, what is it and what can I do about it?

Additional Resources

- PsychCentral.com – "Learning to Let Go of Past Hurts: 5 Ways to Move On"

- HuffPost.com – "When You're Living in the Past"

- BecomingMinimalist.com – "Don't Forget the Past. Learn from It."

- Psychology Today – "3 Definitions of Mindfulness That Might Surprise You"

- Headspace.com – an inexpensive service that uses a smartphone app to help people maximize mindfulness, inner peace, and happiness.

If you would like to look at my bestselling book, "Don't Work Stupid, Coach Yourself," click here.

Chapter 5 (Conclusion):
Living in the Drama-Free Zone

"People talk worse about people than they talk good about people, because a lot of people like drama."

~ Hilary Duff, Actress

One Bite at a Time

How do you eat an Elephant? One bite at a time. And so it is with learning to create and live in a drama-free zone.

There will always be people that love drama and "shaking things up." That will never change. What can change is your response to drama and how you choose to live - either in a zone of drama or in one void of it.

I have presented a lot of different ideas here for how you can create a drama-free zone for yourself, your peers, your manager and employees. If you even adopt a few of these concepts, it will be helpful to you and those around you. You can adopt all of these ideas if you choose, but obviously that will take time. It's a process.

Our world is not getting any simpler nor kinder. Every day we hear about another shooting, a terrible accident, natural disaster, a political firestorm or some other drama. There is so much in the world that will continue to happen regardless of what we do. However, that doesn't mean that we don't have any control in our lives.

One day our granddaughter Kimmy was talking about her first experience working in a restaurant. She said "Opa, people are mean just because they can be. Why don't people be nice?" Why indeed.

I wish you the best of good fortune and a life filled with all kinds of great things, just no drama.

If you ever need to reach out to me, I will be in the drama-free zone.

Chapter Bonus:
Relocation Considerations

"Some places you've been before are so great that you don't ever mind going back. Some places you've been before you don't ever want to go back, you know, like Montreal in the Winter."

~ Morgan Freeman, Actor

Thinking of Relocation?

For anyone thinking of moving for a job, here's a caveat: if the company is in a major metropolitan area and your prospective company has to recruit someone from out of state or far away, there is a reason they cannot find a local candidate. Check out LinkedIn, Indeed.com and Glassdoor reviews and make sure you ask the tough questions in the interview, like what happened to the last 2 people who had this job?

The grass is always greener until you have to water it every day.

For many, relocation is not a drama they want to consider. And yet, there is an opportunity for many people that take a leap of faith and go for it. Sometimes a good relocation can jump start a career in flux.

Beyond that advice: Moving to a different state or part of the country is difficult and complicated. It is a huge undertaking. All factors need to be right or it will not work to your advantage. What factors you ask?

Job

Everything about the job and the company must be right for a period of at least 3 years. Otherwise you will not establish yourself professionally, nor will you have time to create a new business network in your new location. This could mean that if the job does not work out, you may have no choice in what you do for work.

One thing you can do to be sure this opportunity is right you, is to move only yourself for the first 6 months. Live in long-term stay hotels or a small furnished apartment and commute home to family weekends or twice a month. Don't sell your house, nor move your family during that time. After 6 months, if all is well, then move your home and family.

You can easily use the relo money six months later. Also, you will have had time to prove yourself, which could increase the amount of relo money they will pay you. A relocation may be just the opportunity you need to propel your career to the next level.

Another thing to consider is what this relocation will do to your family. Everything will be new and different. They will lose all their friends and acquaintances. This move can cause even the closest of families to experience major drama and change. If you have a family, it's not only about the job for you, it's the whole family package that you should consider.

Salary

Yes, salary is important, but it's also important that the salary is fair for the position and responsibility of the job. If the salary is too high for the job, ask yourself why. Some companies have to pay more because of a difficult company culture, or problem leaders. It's not a matter of you "not being worth that much," it's a matter of a disconnect between job responsibilities and what the company will pay. If it looks too good to be true, find out why.

Some companies offer a normal salary, benefits and high value things like stock options to extract more work and time out of employees' lives for less overall money. They call this "golden handcuffs" - meaning that companies provide all kinds of things (like outrageous stock options, free meals anytime of the day) to keep you at work longer for the same pay. You should ask yourself: What are they going to expect from me? Is it 8 hours a day, 40 hours a week? Or, is it 12 hours a day and a 60 hour work week? It really matters because they are paying for part of your life and there are no refunds if you become dissatisfied.

Nothing is free in this world. Always expect that you will have to pay a price for what you receive. Remember, the only reason to work for a company is how much they pay for part of your life. If the price is not right, consider all your options.

At-Will Employment/Right to Work States

Some states in the U.S. are legally "at-will employment" states. This means that the company can dismiss you for virtually any "legal" reason without notice. If you don't have an employment contract and they let you go, you'll just be out of luck and unemployed with no recourse or income.

It may seem not right or fair, but that's the way the law is in these states. The laws protect the company, not the employee. If you are moving to an "employment at will" state, you need to ask yourself: How secure will this job be? If you don't have an employment contract for several years, the answer is "not very secure."

How can you protect yourself? Get an employment contract in writing for a guaranteed number of years.

Also, right-to-work laws have to do with union and non-union employees and what are their rights. Basically, these laws say that if you're non-union, you can work in union shops with no union membership. States that have this law also tend to remove minimum wage rates.

Depending on your job type, be sure to understand these laws and what this can and cannot do to you.

Career Level

The level of the career is an important consideration for those considering relocation. Here's the reason: At the Director level, you will get some relo money, but not much more. At the VP and above level, you should get a full relo package and an employment contract for several years (typically 3 years).

If the position you are interested in is below a Director level, you should not consider moving for the job, unless you already have a support system in the new area (such as a family). Otherwise, the new area can be a very cold, difficult place.

The exception to this advice is if you are moving anyway for personal reasons, like to be closer to family.

The Company or Organization

You can learn a lot about the company from the Internet. Sites like LinkedIn, Indeed.com and Glassdoor can give you a deep insight into the employee experience, their philosophy, culture, pay, benefits, work-life balance, management, job security and advancement.

The company should be well thought of in their industry by employees, peers and customers. Do you recognize this company and are they a leader in their field? Never relo for a company that is a 2nd or 3rd tier company. They will most likely not get better just because you join them.

Living arrangements

For the first year in a new job (that requires relocation), consider renting a home. There are many reasons for this:

You may hate the job - You move and shortly after starting, you realize that you hate the job. What do you do if you bought a house? You'll most likely need to find another job in the same general area, with no business network established.

You may hate the location - After a month, you realize that something is wrong with the area. It could be the weather, it could be the people, the location, the crime, being in a flood plain. Who knows?

Lack of knowledge of the area - It will take a year for you to learn the area and where you want to live.

Weather Trends - Changing weather patterns are real.

Nothing is predictable anymore. Short-term, the cause is not relevant, only the result. What you need to focus on is how the changing weather pattern affects the area where you decide to live.

Also, you could rent a condo or apartment in an area where you think you'd like to live. This will give you the chance to experience the area with little financial investment or liability.

People at work can be a great source of information about the area to learn which parts are good and which are bad.

Red State/Blue State

Your new state of residence will swing politically one way or the other. Unfortunately, in today's environment, politics is everywhere, and it is vicious, nasty and in your face. It's the very definition of high drama.

The state you live in will reflect a set of social, political, religious and moral values. These values had better be your values, otherwise you will have no friends or acquaintances outside of work and every time your state or city government do something, you will disagree with it.

It doesn't matter what your politics or beliefs. What matters is that those align close enough to the state you will live in, otherwise, you will be miserable.

For example, if you are a conservative and move to Chicago, Illinois area you'll hate the taxes, laws like legal marijuana, unions, cost of living and other things. If you're a liberal and move to Birmingham, Alabama area you will hate the laws, the right-to-work philosophy, the political and religious rhetoric and other things. These are real quality of life issues paramount to your happiness. Choose your state wisely.

Consider this: You now live in either Illinois or Alabama. Would you really want to move to the other state?

There is no reason to move somewhere you will not be happy, unless it is a one year "great adventure." In that case, don't buy a house, rent something. Also, moving for a family is a good reason if you are already familiar with the area.

Culture Shock

While all parts of the United States are tied together by highways, Federal laws, the American English language, television and the Internet, there are very real differences between locations and people. It's important to consider these when looking at a relocation.

Here are some examples:

- Different parts of the country have different diversity. All parts of the country have their own "issues." Some areas will be 80% white, some will be 80% Hispanic-you need to decide whether you will be comfortable with the racial demographic of your chosen location.

- In every state of the union, people drive a different "kind of crazy" on the roads. If the way they drive is not compatible with your driving practices, you will have to adapt. Otherwise, this can cause stress, accidents, as well as an unhappy drive to work and everywhere else.

- Prepared food is blander in the North and spicier in the South. Even snacks are made differently for locations in the United States just as Coca Cola makes its products different for every customer market around the world.

- Midwesterners are very polite, but they will not necessarily tell you what they really think. The good thing is everyone is nice. The bad thing is you won't know if they are being honest with you.

People in New York will speak straight forward and in your face. The good thing is you will know what they are thinking. The bad thing is you may not want to know what they are thinking.

Culture shock is a real consideration when choosing to move to a different part of the country.

Hot vs. Cold Weather and Natural Disasters

If you are from the South, you are used to warmer weather. If you are from the North, you are used to colder weather. When considering a relocation you need to ask yourself if the new climate will be acceptable to you and your family, or whether you will be miserable.

Yes, you can eventually get used to living anywhere. The question is: do you really want to go through that change and settle for living in a place where you hate the weather? For example, if the dark of winter depresses you, would you really want to move to the Arctic circle (Alaska) where there is only 2 hours of daylight for 4 months a year? Granted, that is an extreme example.

Here are some other examples:

- Areas like Seattle, Washington often are raining and cloudy. Sunny days are a rarity.

- Dallas, Texas has lots of sunny days, but also extreme heat in the Spring through the Fall months.

- Minneapolis, Minnesota has sunny days and beautiful lakes during the summers, but the Winters are brutal and so is the average snowfall they receive.

- The temperature and location of the area also dictates the amount of ice and storm that falls in the Winter, the amount of rain during the year, whether there are tornadoes, hurricanes, mudslides, floods, fires and other natural disasters. Oh my.

- Other events like earthquakes, volcanoes happen more often in the western states towards the Pacific coast. Not that earthquakes cannot happen in Illinois, but those are very mild by comparison.

- For someone not accustomed to flash floods, drivers may not know how to drive and what to avoid (low-water crossings) during these types of events.

Climate is an important factor when considering a relocation.

Cost of Living vs. Salary

The salary you make in one location will not be worth the same buying power in a different part of the country. This is a very important issue. There are many websites that will show you what the cost of living is in the new location, compared to your current location.

If you are making $100K a year in Dallas, Texas, and move to Chicago, IL that same salary is only worth about $75K in what it will buy (what things cost). So, the salary should be at least equal in buying power in the new location, preferably higher. Otherwise, you have just moved for the same income. Does that make sense? Consider the cost of selling one's house, packing and moving all your household possessions, buying the new house and all the drama, change and effort you will endure. What is that worth to you? Just selling the old home, buying the new and the move can cost between $20K to $40K (or more).

Taxes

Income, property, sales and other taxes are an important consideration. While only a hand full of states do not have income taxes, property and sales taxes as well as other state and municipal fees can also be a surprise. You should understand these taxes before you move. You do not always get what you pay for in taxes. It's up to you to figure out what is best for your situation.

Schools and Children

If you have children, that means school. Not all school systems or states are created equal for education. The ratings for schools are available online. The question you need to ask: Are the school systems good enough to teach my children? Will I have to put my kids in a private school? If I have to pay for private school is the job salary sufficient to support that?

Also, once children start school, moving to another area will be tough on them, especially if they are teenagers. Moving when children are younger ages 1 to 11 or after they have graduated high school will be less traumatic. The question you need to ask is: When is the right time (if ever) for my family to move?

Family

Relocation across the country or to another state will change a lot of things in your life. One of those changes, potentially, is the relationship you have with the family other than your spouse and children (parents, siblings, cousins, etc) and close friends.

If you've only lived in the same area your whole life, this change will be dramatic. Parents, siblings will only be accessible via phone and video conference. You will see them less, attend fewer graduations and other events and they likewise will take part in less of your life. Even if you try to keep a close relationship with them, it will not be the same. You accept that this is the price you will pay, if you accept a new job that requires relocation.

That's not to say that you should not move for a job or that you can't move back to your original location in a few years. It's really up to you. Each person choses their own path. Just know that the longer you stay in your new location, the less likely it is that you will move back to the original one.

Your Hobbies and Interests

What you do outside of work is just as important as what you do during the workday. It might be more important, if you have a family (spouse and kids).

Your hobbies and interests need to well suited to the new geographical location. For example: if you love culture, such as the symphony, art museums, science venues but you move to the middle of Podunk, how will that help you? You'll be 3 or 4 hours from anything you enjoy. Essentially, you will live in a cultural desert. Unless you love spending all your time at home, it will bore you out of your mind and your kids will have no way to develop culturally.

Likewise, if you are a homebody and love the country life (and things like camping, fishing, hunting and hiking), moving to a densely populated area where the houses are literally touching one another, will make you claustrophobic and you will most likely hate living there (the noise, the smell, the lights, the people, the crime, etc., etc., etc.).

"To each his own," as the saying goes. That's why you need to research where you will live and how well the area aligns with your hobbies and interests.

Mass Transit and Roads

Americans love to drive their cars and trucks. However, access to mass transportation like major airports is important if you have to travel, for vacations and to visit family in other states (if the distance is far).

Access to light rail lines is important if you want to commute to work in the city and not drive and park a car.

The road conditions vary based on the weather, it's extremes, the prosperity of state and local governments and how those roads are constructed and maintained.

Again, these are things to consider in looking at a relocation.

Retirement

If you plan on retiring at your new chosen location, there are other things to consider:

• Whether the state taxes social security income. Some states tax social security benefits, some do not. This is important because the Federal government already taxes it as income. Having the state tax it as well is another expense.

• Real estate tax relief for seniors. Some county tax appraisal districts lock in taxes at a fixed rate when you reach the age of retirement. Having real estate taxes fixed for your property will help offset the continual rise in the cost of living.

• The support system for seniors regarding transportation, medicine, leisure activities. Some places are excellent and provide all kinds of services to seniors. Others do almost nothing.

• Whether the climate will be acceptable to you in old age. Cold climates that have snow and ice can increase the chances of falling and injuries. Southern states can be so hot that heat injury is a genuine concern.

If you are considering a relocation and retirement, consider all the facts for both working and retirement purposes.

Summary

• There are many factors to consider before moving for a job.

• All aspects of the job must be right for 3 years.

- The salary must be appropriate for the position and responsibilities.

- States that are "at-will employment" can be less secure for job holders.

- Directors and above get much better relocation help.

- The state you move to should align with your social, religious and moral values

- Culture shock is real and part of moving to different areas of the country.

- All areas of the country have different weather problems and issues.

- The cost of living differs by state.

- Your salary should be higher in buying power at the new location.

- Every state has different taxes and tax rates.

- Once children start school, it is more difficult to move.

- Being separated from other family and friends is the price you pay for the new opportunity and location.

- Your hobbies and interests should align with the new location.

- If you are planning on retiring in the new location, it should be an area that has a high quality of life for seniors.

Questions to Ask Yourself

- Why is this company willing to move someone from across the country? Why can't they find a person locally? Have I checked out the company well?

- Will this job be right for me? Will it be stable for 3 years?

- What effect will the relocation have on my family?

- Is the salary right for the position and responsibilities? If not, why is it so high (or low)?

- Am I moving to an "employment at will" state? If yes, how can I protect myself?

- What do employees, peers and customers think of this company I will work for?

- Am I willing to rent for a year, rather than buy a house in the new area?

- Does the new location align with my social, political, religious and moral values?

- If I experience culture shock how will I adapt? Do I want to adapt?

- Is the weather in the new location acceptable long term for me and my family?

- Is the cost of living in the new location affordable, based on the new salary?

- Do I understand all the taxes and fees charged in the new area?

- Are the schools in the new location acceptable to educate my children?

- Am I willing to reduce or lose some relationships with family and friends for this new job?

- Does the new area align with my hobbies and interests, or is it a total mismatch?

- Is mass transit available in the new area? What is the condition of the roads in the area?

- Is this state retirement friendly for seniors?

Can I Ask You a Favor?

Would you write a brief review about what you think about this book on Amazon.com? It would really help people find this book, and I read all the reviews. Here is the web address: https://www.amazon.com/dp/B07Z5F1LMR

Thank you.

Don't Forget

Don't Forget about the free materials: it's a hyperlinked list of additional resources you can read on each subject discussed in this book and other free tools.

You can download this file for free on my website. (https://coachyourselfbooks.com/worksheets/)

About the Author

Mark Baggesen has been a manager, writer and mentor to over 100 people for the last 25 years. He is an expert at turning chaos into success, recovering failed technology projects and complex problem solving.

In this book, Mark is hoping to have people question their interactions with others in the workplace. He believes that working from a point of civility, empathy and knowledge, people can make themselves and others happier.

He lives in the northwest suburbs of Chicago with his family.

<u>Notes</u>

www.ingramcontent.com/pod-product-compliance
Lightning Source LLC
Chambersburg PA
CBHW021439210526
45463CB00002B/581